THE *New Jersey* COLONY

Our Thirteen Colonies

SPIRIT
of America®

THE *New Jersey* COLONY

By Myra S. Weatherly

Content Adviser: Eric Gilg, Department of History, University of
Massachusetts, Amherst, Massachusetts

The Child's World®
Chanhassen, Minnesota

6

THE *New Jersey* COLONY

Published in the United States of America by The Child's World®
PO Box 326 • Chanhassen, MN 55317-0326 • 800-599-READ • www.childsworld.com

Acknowledgments
The Child's World®: Mary Berendes, Publishing Director

Editorial Directions, Inc.: E. Russell Primm, Editorial Director; Melissa McDaniel, Line Editor; Elizabeth K. Martin, Assistant Editor; Olivia Nellums, Editorial Assistant; Susan Hindman, Copy Editor; Joanne Mattern, Proofreader; Kevin Cunningham, Peter Garnham, Ruthanne Swiatkowski, Fact Checkers; Tim Griffin/IndexServ, Indexer; Cian Loughlin O'Day, Photo Researcher; Linda S. Koutris, Photo Selector

Photo
Cover: North Wind Picture Archives; Bettmann/Corbis: 16, 25, 29; Corbis: 6, 9 (Richard T. Nowitz), 12, 19, 28, 33, 35; Getty Images/ Hulton Archive: 11, 13, 17, 21, 22, 23, 26, 27, 32, 34; New Jersey State Archives, Department of State: 8, 14, 20, 30; North Wind Picture Archives: 15, 18; Stock Montage: 24.

Library of Congress Cataloging-in-Publication Data
Weatherly, Myra.
 The New Jersey colony / by Myra S. Weatherly.
   p. cm. — (Our colonies)
"Spirit of America."
Includes bibliographical references (p.) and index.
Contents: The Lenni-Lenape people—Coming of the Europeans—A fractured colony—Crossroads of the American Revolution—The Garden State—Time line—Glossary terms.
 ISBN 1-56766-624-8 (alk. paper)
 1. New Jersey—History—Colonial period, ca. 1600–1775—Juvenile literature. 2. New Jersey—History—1775–1865—Juvenile literature. [1. New Jersey—History—Colonial period, ca. 1600–1775. 2. New Jersey—History—1775–1865.] I. Title. II. Series.
 F137.W37 2003
 974.9'02—dc21   2003003772

Contents

Chapter ONE

The Lenni-Lenape People

The Delaware River marks the boundary between New Jersey and the state of Pennsylvania to the west.

PEOPLE LIVED IN WHAT WOULD BECOME NEW Jersey for thousands of years before Europeans arrived there. By the time the first Europeans saw the region, the Lenni-Lenape people were living there.

The Lenni-Lenape lived in villages of about 600 people. Each family lived in a home called a wigwam. The men cut young trees to make these houses. They stood the trees in the ground to form a circle. Then they tied the tops together with leather strips, leaving a hole for smoke from cooking fires to escape. Finally, they covered the frame with bark and grass.

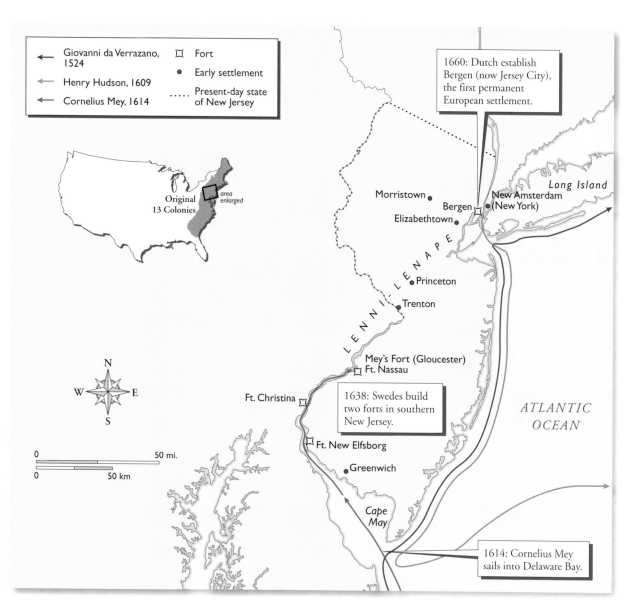

The Lenni-Lenape hunted and trapped deer, elk, and beaver. They cut trails through the towering forests that led from villages to hunting and fishing grounds. They fished with huge nets, some as long as 500 feet (150 meters). They rowed through the rivers in big canoes that could carry 40 people.

New Jersey Colony at the time of the first European settlement

7

The Lenni-Lenape were skilled hunters and fishers. The canoes they carved from huge tree trunks were important to their success in these activities.

While the men hunted, fished, and made tools and weapons, the women also kept busy. They raised crops and gathered nuts and berries from the forests and shellfish from the coast. The women worked animal skins into clothing and blankets. They also made pottery.

The Lenni-Lenape played as hard as they worked, whether stomp-dancing to the beat of a water drum or playing Lenni-Lenape football. In football, the men played against the women, using a ball made of deerskin and stuffed with deer hair. The Lenni-Lenape also loved storytelling. As they carried on their daily activities, the Lenni-Lenape had no way of knowing that in the years ahead, their lifestyle would vanish.

8

To make a cone-shaped pot, Lenni-Lenape women first cleaned the clay of sticks and pebbles. They added water to make the clay workable. They also mixed crushed stone or shell with the clay to prevent the pot from cracking during the firing.

After working and pressing the clay, the women formed it into a rope. To achieve a cone shape, they dug a small hole in the ground and lined it with soft grass. Starting at the base of the hole, they coiled the rope, layer upon layer. After finishing the coils, they took the pot out and smoothed the outside. Then they decorated the pot with designs and put it in the sun to dry. The women made the pot hard through the process of firing, filling the pot with hot coals and building a fire around it. The Lenni-Lenape used their clay pots for cooking or storing food.

9

Chapter Two

The Europeans Arrive

Like Giovanni da Verrazano, Englishman Henry Hudson sailed along the coast of what is now New Jersey, in the ship shown here.

IN 1524, ITALIAN EXPLORER GIOVANNI DA Verrazano and his crew became the first Europeans to drop anchor off what would become New Jersey. They were searching for a sailing route to Asia. Curious Lenni-Lenape greeted the visitors. Verrazano wrote to the king of France, who had paid for the trip, "They came without fear aboard our ship."

Eighty-five years later, a small ship named *Half Moon,* under the command of English explorer Henry Hudson, anchored in Newark Bay. Hudson was also searching for a sailing route to Asia. According to

Hudson, the Lenni-Lenape who brought his crew oysters, corn, and fruits were "civil and kind." One of the ship's officers, Robert Juet, wrote that the region was "a very good land to fall in with, and a pleasant land to see." Before returning to Europe, Hudson sailed up what is now the Hudson River.

Because the Dutch had funded Hudson's voyage, they claimed the area he had explored. This area included much of what is now New York and New Jersey. The Dutch founded a colony called New Netherland, which attracted fur trappers and settlers. In 1614, Dutch explorer Cornelius Mey sailed into Delaware Bay with three ships. He established a small fort in southwestern New Jersey. Cape May bears his name, with a slight change in spelling.

Henry Hudson noted that the Lenni-Lenape were the kindest and most civilized natives he encountered during his travels on the Half Moon.

11

Most early Europeans considered many Native American customs and traditions strange, especially the art of body painting, or tattooing.

Many Dutch fur trappers and traders tramped onto the shores of the Delaware River in the early 1630s. The Dutch traded pots, guns, blankets, and rum to the Lenni-Lenape for valuable furs.

The Lenni-Lenape offered food and shelter to the strangers, and the newcomers found them friendly. But the Europeans didn't understand some Lenni-Lenape traditions. They thought it strange that the Native Americans coated their hair with fish oil, painted their faces, and tattooed their chests with serpent images.

In 1638, the fur trade brought Swedes to New Jersey. They built forts along the banks of the Delaware River. But Dutch soldiers, led by one-legged Peter Stuyvesant, the governor of New Netherland, took over the New Sweden colony in 1655. Five years later, the

Dutch established New Jersey's first permanent town, Bergen, which is now called Jersey City.

Long before the Dutch established New Netherland, the British had settled along the Atlantic coast of North America. In 1664, the British seized New Netherland from the Dutch. The English king, Charles II, gave the region to his brother James, Duke of York, renaming it New York. James granted Englishmen Lord John Berkeley and Sir George Carteret control of the southern part of the region. They named the land New Jersey for Jersey, an island in the English Channel. Because Berkeley and Carteret were in charge of the colony, they were called the **proprietors** of New Jersey.

Peter Stuyvesant lost his leg while serving as a governor in the West Indies. His replacement leg was wooden with silver bands, which gave rise to the legend that he wore a silver leg.

CONTACT WITH THE DUTCH HAD A HUGE EFFECT ON THE LENNI-LENAPE. The Native Americans had been friendly to their new neighbors. They taught the Europeans how to use fish for fertilizer, preserve food, and make bread from corn. They also taught the Dutch to treat wounds and illnesses using plants. The friendly relations changed between 1640 and 1650, as settlers began claiming lands where the Lenni-Lenape had long lived.

Disease, warfare, and loss of land all hurt the Lenni-Lenape. The Europeans had brought new diseases to the Americas. The Native Americans had never before been exposed to these diseases, so their bodies could not fight them. Thousands of Lenni-Lenape died, and millions of Native Americans died throughout North America. Wars between Native Ameri-

cans and conflicts with the settlers caused more deaths. Also, the fur trade had led to a sharp decline in the animal population. Many Lenni-Lenape died of starvation, because there were not enough animals to hunt. Others were forced to trade their land for food and clothing and head west. In the early 1600s, about 12,000 Lenni-Lenape lived in what is now New Jersey. By 1700, there were less than 2,500.

Chapter THREE

A Fractured Colony

When Philip Carteret first arrived on the shores of New Jersey, he already felt a sense of ownership of the land. This attitude caused problems with settlers who had been living there long before Carteret had appeared.

THE GOVERNOR OF NEW YORK DID not know that James, Duke of York, had granted New Jersey to Carteret and Berkeley. The governor was giving land in New Jersey to settlers from New York and Long Island. Carteret and Berkeley tried to make these people pay them rent. This rent caused a number of riots. Despite the conflicts, the colony flourished.

The proprietors set up a **charter** for governing the colony. The charter gave New Jersey colonists religious freedom and some say in governing the colony. Under the charter, the government would be run by an appointed governor and an **assembly** of 12, chosen by the people.

16

In 1665, Carteret chose his nephew, Philip Carteret, to be governor of New Jersey. Philip, who was living in England at the time, and about 30 English settlers sailed across the Atlantic. This group settled at Elizabethtown. Dissatisfied settlers in New England also moved to New Jersey. Most were **Puritans** who had fled to North America because they opposed the Church of England, the official church there.

In the mid-1600s, England saw much conflict over who would rule the land. When the kings were restored to power, the Puritan religion was outlawed. Many Puritans fled to America seeking freedom and safety.

17

This meeting house in Burlington, New Jersey, was built in 1683 by members of the First Society of Friends, or Quakers. The Quakers had a large role in the settlement and early government of New Jersey.

The New Jersey General Assembly first met in Elizabethtown in 1668. They passed many strict laws. Disobeying these laws resulted in public whippings.

New Jersey's early colonists found life harsh. They lived in huts or caves before building houses. Their vegetable gardens provided food. Farming, hunting, and fishing became a way of life for them. From an early age, children helped with household chores and farming.

The colony had no public schools. Children attended small private schools or were taught by tutors. In 1746, New Jersey established a college in Elizabethtown for training ministers. Ten years later, the college moved to Princeton. It became Princeton University.

In the course of its early history, New Jersey passed from owner to owner. Needing money, Lord Berkeley sold his half of New Jersey in 1674 to English **Quakers** named Edward Billing and John Fenwick. In 1676,

the Quaker proprietors and Sir George Carteret, who was still the colony's other proprietor, agreed to divide New Jersey into two parts—West Jersey and East Jersey. Under the plan, East Jersey would remain a Puritan stronghold. West Jersey went to the peace-loving Quakers. A few years later, East Jersey was also sold to the Quakers.

William Penn, Pennsylvania's founder, helped organize Quaker settlements in West Jersey. He wrote a second charter for that area, stating that "we put the power in the people." West Jersey served as a safe place for English, Irish, Welsh, and Scottish Quakers who had been treated badly in their own countries. Members of other religious groups also settled there. Many Germans started new lives in New Jersey. The two Jerseys were finally combined into one colony in 1702.

Princeton University's Nassau Hall (left) and the President's House (now called Maclean House) are both listed in official records as having been built in 1756.

Interesting Fact

▸ America's first successful glass factory, the Wistarburgh Glass Works, opened in Alloway Township, Salem County, New Jersey, in 1739. Some of the pieces made by this factory are housed today at the Museum of American Glass, in Millville, New Jersey.

New industries, such as shipbuilding, iron-making, and glassmaking, flourished in the colony, spurring the growth of towns. New Jersey's fertile soil was good for farming. In the western part of the colony, people owned large farms called plantations. The owners used slave labor to operate these farms. The Dutch had brought enslaved Africans to New Jersey when they arrived in the 1620s, but there were also Native American slaves in the colony. By 1750, about 6,000 of New Jersey's 71,000 people were enslaved.

Enslaved workers helped build the colony. They labored long hours at backbreaking jobs for no money. Breaking the rules led to brutal whippings. Those who dared to run away were cruelly punished if captured.

Unlike many Northern states, New Jersey was slow in outlawing slavery. The Quakers did not believe in owning slaves, but most other people in New Jersey favored allowing slavery. Slavery did not begin to decline in New Jersey until the 1830s.

As the colony grew in size, publishing was among the many new businesses that became important. The New Jersey Gazette *was one of the earliest newspapers in the American colonies.*

IN THE LATE 1690S AND EARLY 1700S, PIRATES SWARMED THE NEW JERSEY coast. The coastline's many inlets became hiding places for pirate ships and, some say, for pirate loot.

One of the most famous pirates of the time was Captain William Kidd. He was put on trial and found guilty of being a pirate. On May 23, 1701, his lifeless body, covered with tar and bound with chains, was hung over the Thames River in London, England. It remained there until it rotted away, as a warning to future pirates. Kidd's life had ended, but his name became legendary.

On his final voyage, Captain Kidd had anchored near Sandy Hook, New Jersey. Rumors that he had hidden a huge stash of money there sent fortune hunters to New Jersey's shores. After much digging for buried treasure over the centuries, only a few gold coins have ever been found. However, some people still search the New Jersey coast for Kidd's plunder.

Chapter FOUR

Crossroads of the Revolution

King George III of England and the British Parliament began imposing taxes on the American colonists to help pay for the French and Indian War.

DURING THE 18TH CENTURY, FRANCE AND Great Britain competed for control of the rich farmland and fur trade in the Ohio River valley, to the west of New Jersey. In 1754, this competition turned into the French and Indian War. By the time the fighting ended in 1763, the British had won control of Canada and lands east of the Mississippi River.

The war left Great Britain heavily in debt. To raise money, British Parliament imposed taxes on the colonists for shipped sugar, paper, tea, and other goods. These taxes angered the colonists, who began protesting. In 1773, Massachusetts colonists snuck aboard three ships in Boston Harbor and dumped trunks of tea in the

water to protest the tea tax. This became known as the Boston Tea Party.

Delegates from the colonies came together as the First **Continental Congress** in Philadelphia, Pennsylvania, in the summer of 1774. They hoped to find a peaceful solution to the crisis with Britain. But tensions only grew worse.

Months later, New Jersey held its own "tea party." A group of New Jersey men dressed as Native Americans burned a shipload of British tea in the town of Greenwich.

Reception at the Governor's Mansion in New Jersey; New Jersey Governor William Franklin, son of Benjamin Franklin, was opposed to breaking from England.

When George Washington left his wife, Martha, with a promise to return soon, he didn't expect to be gone several years. But without his wisdom and courage, the Revolutionary War may have turned out differently.

In April 1775, the first shots of the American Revolution were fired at the Battle of Lexington and Concord in Massachusetts. The colonies were on the brink of a full-scale war, but they had no army and no navy to fight the mighty British forces. The Continental Congress met again and created a national army of ordinary men, not professional soldiers. When George Washington took on the job of commanding the army, he wrote to his wife, Martha, that he would "return safe to you in the fall." But his safe return home would be eight and a half years later.

In the spring of 1776, the Second Continental Congress discussed a vital question: Should the

13 colonies become a separate nation? The delegates decided the answer was yes. On July 4, 1776, they adopted the Declaration of Independence, which said the 13 colonies were now "the thirteen United States of America." Freedom had been declared—but it still had to be won.

Washington always took the time to pray for safety and victory with his troops.

Wedged between New York City and Philadelphia, New Jersey played a central role in the American Revolution. Almost 100 battles took place on this little piece of land between 1775 and 1783.

In late 1776, British forces took control of most of New Jersey, forcing Washington and his troops to flee into Pennsylvania. German soldiers hired by the British, called Hessians, guarded the captured towns. They never expected the ragged and weary American troops to return.

On the night of December 25, 1776, Washington ordered the troops across the ice-clogged Delaware River. As the army started

Interesting Fact

▶ So many troops moved through New Jersey en route to New York and Pennsylvania, during America's fight for independence that New Jersey came to be known as the "crossroads of the American Revolution." More battles were fought there than in any other colony, but South Carolina ranks a close second.

General Washington parades the Hessian soldiers captured in Trenton through the streets of Philadelphia.

across, John Fitzgerald, Washington's aide, wrote: "It is fearfully cold and raw and a snowstorm is setting in. . . . It will be a terrible night for those who have no shoes, . . . but I have not heard a man complain."

The following morning, the troops moved quietly into Trenton, forcing the surprised Hessians south. Firing from the upper stories of houses and from behind woodpiles, Washington's troops kept the Hessians from moving back into the city. Only a few of Washington's men were injured. The victory encouraged hundreds of New Jerseyans to join the army.

On January 3, 1777, Washington drove the British from Princeton in another surprise attack. This time, the Americans wrapped their horses' hooves and their cannon wheels with rags so they could move silently. After the battle at Princeton, the Continental army camped at Morristown for the winter.

On June 28, 1778, the American army of about 13,000 men led by Washington clashed with the British forces at the New Jersey town of Monmouth Courthouse. Sir Henry Clinton commanded some 10,000 British troops. This was the biggest one-day battle of the war, but neither side could claim victory. Washington held the field, but the British sneaked away to New York during

General Washington's successful surprise attack on Princeton, New Jersey, in January, 1777, proved to many that he was an imaginative and daring leader.

27

the night. The war would continue for another three years.

In August 1781, Washington again marched his troops through New Jersey, this time on the way to Yorktown, Virginia. The American victory at Yorktown marked the end of the fighting. In 1783, the United States and Great Britain signed a peace treaty.

In October, 1781, British General Lord Cornwallis surrendered to George Washington at Yorktown, as depicted in this painting. Here, the French navy surrounds the fallen troops.

DURING THE AMERICAN REVOLUTION, IT WAS COMMON FOR WOMEN TO TRAVEL with the Continental army. They tended to wounded soldiers and brought food and drink to men in battle. Mary Hays was the wife of officer William Hays. Mary went with her husband everywhere, including to the freezing camp at Valley Forge, Pennsylvania, and to the battlefield at Monmouth Courthouse, New Jersey.

At Monmouth, Mary earned the nickname Molly Pitcher. There, on a scorching hot day, she ran back and forth across the bullet-swept ground to a nearby spring. She brought pitcher after pitcher of water to the exhausted men and to help cool the cannons. Over and over, she heard the cry, "Molly, pitcher!"

Popular legend says that when William Hays fell to the ground wounded, Mary took her husband's place at the cannon and fired it. She manned the gun for the rest of the battle.

29

Chapter FIVE

The New Nation

Broad and Market Streets in colonial Trenton were part of a lively business district. But with little established order in the new national government, New Jersey and other new states still had many problems to face.

THE 13 COLONIES HAD WON THEIR INDEPEN-dence, but the country was far from united. Although some states were strong, the national government was in shambles. Under the nation's first **constitution,** called the **Articles**

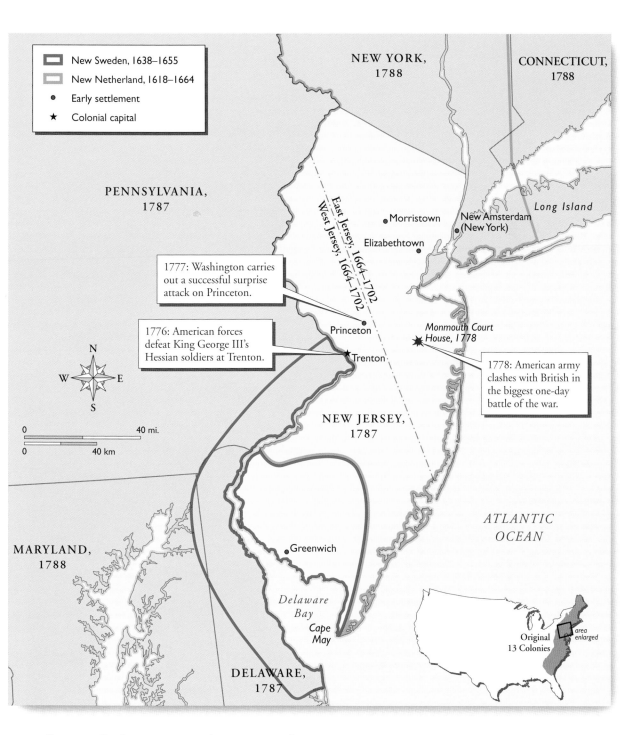

Legend:

- New Sweden, 1638–1655
- New Netherland, 1618–1664
- Early settlement
- Colonial capital

NEW YORK, 1788

CONNECTICUT, 1788

PENNSYLVANIA, 1787

East Jersey, 1664–1702
West Jersey, 1664–1702

Long Island

Morristown

New Amsterdam (New York)

Elizabethtown

1777: Washington carries out a successful surprise attack on Princeton.

1776: American forces defeat King George III's Hessian soldiers at Trenton.

Princeton

Monmouth Court House, 1778

Trenton

1778: American army clashes with British in the biggest one-day battle of the war.

N W E S

0 40 mi.
0 40 km

NEW JERSEY, 1787

ATLANTIC OCEAN

MARYLAND, 1788

Greenwich

Delaware Bay

Cape May

DELAWARE, 1787

Original 13 Colonies

area enlarged

New Jersey Colony before statehood

of Confederation, the central government had little power. It did not even have enough money to pay government bills. The new

31

nation also lacked a permanent capital. During the 1780s, Princeton and Trenton each served briefly as the nation's capital. Between 1776 and 1800, the capital changed location 10 times before finally settling in Washington, D.C.

By 1787, it was clear that the government wasn't working. Delegates met in Philadelphia to come up with a new constitution to govern the nation. Various plans were discussed during the summer of 1787.

After the Revolutionary War, more stability came to the developing cities and to government. Here, the young town of Hoboken looks peaceful and far-removed from bustling New York City in the background.

Philadelphia's sweltering heat did not stop the delegates from holding their talks in secret—behind closed doors and windows.

Delegate William Patterson presented the New Jersey Plan at the meeting. This plan would have given each state an equal

The delegates met secretly to come up with a new constitution to guide the new nation as it grew. This document replaced the Articles of Confederation

During the Revolutionary War, William Paterson was attorney general of New Jersey. After the war he was chosen to be part of the group that laid out the new country's constitution.

number of votes in a one-house Congress, regardless of a state's population. But states with large populations thought this would give small states too much power. The New Jersey Plan was defeated. Instead, the delegates agreed on a two-house Congress, which is what we have today. The number of members each state gets in the House of Representatives is based on its population. In the Senate, however, each state has two votes.

Some people worried that the new Constitution gave the government too much power. Their concerns were answered by adding a list of personal rights to the Constitution. This list, called the Bill of Rights, guarantees Americans many rights, including freedom of religion and freedom of speech.

Nine states had to approve the new U.S. Constitution before it went into effect. On December 18, 1787, New Jersey delegates met in Trenton and voted to approve it. With that vote, New Jersey—home of the Lenni-Lenape and scene of three major revolutionary battles—became the third state of the United States of America.

The first president, George Washington, is received in Trenton amid celebration on April 21, 1789.

Time LINE

1524   1655   1777

1524 Giovanni da Verrazano becomes the first European to explore the New Jersey coast.

1609 Englishman Henry Hudson explores New Jersey.

1614 Dutch explorer Cornelius Mey sails into Delaware Bay.

1630s Dutch fur trappers arrive in New Jersey.

1638 Swedes build two forts in southern New Jersey.

1655 Peter Stuyvesant takes control of the New Sweden colony.

1660 The Dutch establish Bergen (now Jersey City), the first permanent European settlement in New Jersey.

1664 England gains control of New Jersey.

1676 The colony is divided into East Jersey and West Jersey.

1702 East Jersey and West Jersey are united as one colony.

1774 Protesters burn a shipload of British tea in the town of Greenwich.

1776 The Declaration of Independence is signed; the Continental army wins the Battle of Trenton.

1777 George Washington leads a successful surprise attack on British forces at Princeton.

1787 New Jersey becomes the third state when it approves the U.S. Constitution.

36

Glossary TERMS

**Articles of Confederation
(AR-tih-kuhlz of kuhn-fed-er-AY-shun)**
The Articles of Confederation was the first constitution of the United States. The Articles of Confederation was replaced by the U.S. Constitution in 1788.

assembly (uh-SEM-blee)
An assembly is a lawmaking part of a government. The first New Jersey General Assembly met in 1668.

charter (CHAR-tur)
A charter is a document setting up a colony. The first New Jersey charter gave settlers religious freedom and some say freedom in governing the colony.

constitution (kon-stuh-TOO-shun)
A constitution is a document outlining the structure and basic laws of a government. The U.S. Constitution replaced the Articles of Confederation in 1788.

**Continental Congress
(kon-tuh-NEN-tuhl KONG-riss)**
The Continental Congress was a meeting of colonists that served as the American government during Revolutionary times. The Second Continental Congress adopted the Declaration of Independence in 1776.

delegates (DEL-uh-guhts)
Delegates are people who represent other people at a meeting. New Jersey sent five delegates to the Continental Congress.

proprietors (pruh-PRY-uh-tuhrs)
Proprietors were people given ownership of a colony. John Berkeley and George Carteret were the first two proprietors of New Jersey.

Puritans (PYOOR-uh-tuhns)
Puritans were American colonists who wanted a stricter, "purer" form of religion than was practiced in England. Many Puritans settled in eastern New Jersey.

Quakers (KWAY-kurs)
The Quakers were a religious group that opposed war and believed that everyone is equal before God. Many Quakers settled in New Jersey.

New Jersey Colony's FOUNDING FATHERS

David Brearley (1741–1790)
New Jersey state supreme court associate justice, 1779–89; Constitutional Convention delegate, 1787; U.S. Constitution signer; U.S. district court justice for New Jersey, 1789–90

Abraham Clark (1726–1794)
Continental Congress delegate, 1776–78, 1779–83; 1787–89; Declaration of Independence signer; U.S. House of Representatives member, 1791–94

Jonathan Dayton (1760–1824)
Constitutional Convention delegate, 1787; U.S. Constitution signer; Continental Congress delegate, 1787–89; U.S. House of Representatives member, 1791–99; U.S. House of Representatives speaker, 1795–99; U.S. senator, 1799–1805; New Jersey state assembly member, 1814–15

John Hart (ca. 1711–1779)
Continental Congress delegate, 1776; Declaration of Independence signer; New Jersey Council of Safety chairman, 1777–78

Francis Hopkinson (1737–1791)
Continental Congress delegate, 1776; Declaration of Independence signer; helped design U.S. flag; U.S. district court justice, eastern Pennsylvania district, 1790

William Churchill Houston (ca. 1746–1788)
Continental Congress delegate, 1779–81, 1784–85; Constitutional Convention delegate, 1787

William Livingston (1723–1790)
Continental Congress delegate, 1774–76; New Jersey governor, 1776–90; Constitutional Convention delegate, 1787; U.S. Constitution signer

William Paterson (1745–1806)
New Jersey attorney general, 1776–83; Constitutional Convention delegate, 1787; U.S. Constitution signer; U.S. senator, 1789–90; New Jersey governor, 1790–93; U.S. supreme court associate justice, 1793–1806

Nathaniel Scudder (1733–1781)
Continental Congress delegate, 1777–79; Articles of Confederation signer

Richard Stockton (1730–1781)
New Jersey state supreme court associate justice, 1774–76; Continental Congress delegate, 1776; Declaration of Independence signer

John Witherspoon (1723–1794)
Continental Congress delegate, 1776–79, 1780–81, 1782; Declaration of Independence signer; Articles of Confederation signer; New Jersey state legislature member, 1783

For Further INFORMATION

Web Sites

Visit our homepage for lots of links about the New Jersey colony:
http://www.childsworld.com/links.html

Note to Parents, Teachers, and Librarians:
We routinely verify our Web links to make sure they're safe,
active sites—so encourage your readers to check them out!

Books

Cuyler, Margery. *The Battlefield Ghost.* New York: Scholastic, 2002.

Fritz, Jean. *Shh! We're Writing the Constitution.* New York: Putnam, 1987.

King, David C. *Revolutionary War Days: Discover the Past with Exciting Games, Activities, and Recipes.* New York: John Wiley & Sons, 2001.

Rockwell, Anne. *They Called Her Molly Pitcher.* New York: Alfred A. Knopf, 2002.

Stefoff, Rebecca. *The Colonies.* New York: Marshall Cavendish, 2001.

Places to Visit or Contact

Indian King Tavern Museum
To visit a tavern that served as an important meeting place during the Revolutionary War
233 Kings Highway East
Haddonfield, NJ 08033
856/429-6792

Washington Crossing State Park
To visit the spot where George Washington and his troops landed after crossing the icy Delaware River in preparation for their surprise attack on Trenton
355 Washington-Crossing-Pennington Road
Titusville, NJ 08560
609/737-0623

Index

About the Author

MYRA WEATHERLY IS THE AUTHOR OF MANY BOOKS FOR CHILDREN and young adults, including *Women Pirates: Eight Stories of Adventure, William Marshal: Medieval England's Greatest Knight, Dolley Madison: America's First Lady,* and *The Taj Mahal.* She has also written *Tennessee, South Carolina,* and *Nebraska* in the America the Beautiful series, as well as *The Thirteen Colonies: New Jersey.* In addition to her writing, Weatherly enjoys sharing her books with young people, traveling, and reading.